With Open Hands

With Open Hands

A Story about Biddy Mason

by Jeri Chase Ferris
illustrated by Ralph L. Ramstad

A Creative Minds Biography

🌿 Carolrhoda Books, Inc./Minneapolis

In honor of America's brave pioneer women of all colors, and for America's children

The author wishes to thank Linda Brown, Biddy Mason's descendant; Bobi Jackson, historian; Sandra Kamusikiri, Ph.D.; Miriam Matthews and Charles Matthews; Rev. Paulette Seagraves, FAME archivist; LeAnne von Neumeyer-Hull, Mormon Family History Research Center, Los Angeles; Brent A. Wood, Ph.D.; my editor, Gwenyth Swain; my husband, Tom; and librarians everywhere.

This book is available in two editions:
Library binding by Carolrhoda Books, Inc.,
    a division of Lerner Publishing Group
Soft cover by First Avenue Editions,
    an imprint of Lerner Publishing Group
241 First Avenue North
Minneapolis, MN 55401 U.S.A.

Website address: www.lernerbooks.com

Library of Congress Cataloging-in-Publication Data

Ferris, Jeri.
    With open hands : a story about Biddy Mason / by Jeri Chase Ferris ; illustrations by Ralph L. Ramstad.
        p.   cm.   — (A creative minds biography)
    Includes bibliographical references and index.
    Summary: Recounts the life of Biddy Mason, a slave who found freedom in California in 1856, who practiced the philosophy of sharing as she nursed the sick, delivered babies, and started many philanthropic projects after becoming a wealthy landowner in Los Angeles.
    ISBN 1-57505-330-6 (lib. bdg. : alk. paper)
    ISBN 0-87614-845-3 (pbk. : alk. paper)
    1. Mason, Biddy, 1818-1891—Juvenile literature. 2. Women slaves—United States—Biography—Juvenile literature. 3. Slaves—United States—Biography—Juvenile literature. 4. Afro-American women—Biography—Juvenile literature. 5. Afro-American midwives—California—Biography—Juvenile literature. [1. Mason, Biddy, 1818-1891. 2. Slaves. 3. Afro-Americans—Biography. 4. Women—Biography.] I. Ramstad, Ralph L., 1919- ill. II. Title. III. Series.
E444.M38F47   1999
973'.0496073'0092—dc21
                                                                                        98-16247

Manufactured in the United States of America
2 3 4 5 6 7 — MA — 06 05 04 03 02 01

Table of Contents

Foreword   6

Introduction   7

A Slave Girl   9

Leaving Mississippi   14

Crossing the Prairie   27

To California and Freedom   35

On Her Own   43

With Open Hands   54

Afterword   59

Bibliography   60

Index   62

About the Author   64

About the Illustrator   64

Foreword
by
Linda Spikes Cox Brown

This is the story of my great-great-great-grandmother, Biddy Mason. As you read her story, you will realize what a remarkable woman she was. It's hard for me to imagine being born in slavery and even harder to imagine my children being someone's slaves. I think of the difficulties Biddy had to endure. I envision the many miles she walked while taking care of her slave owners, their children, her own children, and the animals. Could I have done it? Probably not.

Biddy Mason, through all her trials and tribulations, loved people and kept a positive attitude. Once she was free, she thought only of how she could continue to help others as she had always done. When I think of heroines, Biddy is first in my mind. Sometimes when I'm feeling down, I even touch a copy of the papers that were given to Biddy when the court freed her from slavery. This seems to put me closer to her, and I feel better. Suddenly I realize that I am truly blessed.

Although Biddy died over one hundred years ago and I never knew her, she has always been with me. Her philosophy of helping others was instilled in me by my father, Robert Owens Spikes (Biddy's great-great-grandson) and by my grandmother, Gladys Owens Smith (Biddy's great-granddaughter). I hope that I have given these same values to my children, Cheryl and Robynn Cox. The legacy of our family began with Biddy Mason, who gave to others with open hands.

Introduction

Biddy Mason was born a slave in Georgia in 1818—just one of millions of Southern slaves. But Biddy's life was different from that of other slaves. She became one of the richest women in Southern California.

Biddy Mason gave her riches with open hands to anyone in need, whether black, white, or brown. "The open hand is blessed," she said, "for it gives in abundance, even as it receives."

Biddy could not write the story of her life, but others wrote about her and remembered her giving ways. This story is taken from the journals of those who traveled with her, from documents in Los Angeles, and from family history.

1

A Slave Girl

Biddy Mason was born in Hancock County, Georgia, on August 15, 1818. Her slave name was Bridget, but everyone called her Biddy. She had no last name.

Biddy never knew her mother or her father. She was still a very little girl when she was taken from her mother and given to the slave-owning family of John Smithson. Her mother wasn't asked to give up her child, any more than a cow is "asked" to give up its calf. Perhaps Biddy was sold for a sack of tobacco leaves, or traded for a debt due, or given away as a present to the Smithsons. Nobody knows.

The Smithsons took Biddy with them to Mississippi and put her in with their other slaves. The slaves gave the little girl a space on the dirt floor of a wood cabin. They cared for her and taught her everything she needed to know.

Biddy learned how a slave must behave toward her master and toward the master's wife and children. She learned how to cook and clean, scrub floors and sweep out fireplaces, wash grimy clothes and dirty dishes. She learned to keep working even when it was so hot the dogs lay panting in the shade, and heavy moss hung limply from the trees.

By the time Biddy was a teenager, she knew as much about treating fevers and sore throats and sick stomachs as any of the women who had taught her. She knew where to look in the woods for just the right herbs and plants to make her medicines, and she was happy to help make other people, black or white, feel better again.

She knew how to make soap and how to boil clothes in a huge kettle over the fire. She knew how to bake yams and biscuits in a Dutch oven. She knew how to take care of the master's house. She even knew how to help a mother having a baby.

There were two things Biddy did not know, however. She did not know how to read and she did not know how to write. She wasn't *allowed* to know, for it was against the law for anyone to teach a slave such dangerous skills. After all, a slave who could read might learn how to get free. So Biddy learned how to do things with her hands.

When Biddy was eighteen years old, she was given away again. Mr. Smithson's cousin Rebecca married Robert M. Smith in 1836, and the Smithsons needed to give a generous gift. They chose to give Biddy, who was hardy and strong, along with three other slaves as their wedding present to Rebecca and Robert Smith.

Biddy took all her possessions: an extra, well-patched dress, a blanket, her collection of plants and herbs wrapped in a cloth. Perhaps she even took an old rag doll from childhood.

Robert Smith was kind enough, Biddy saw, but his new wife was a sickly thing. Biddy was soon spending most of her time caring for the frail Rebecca Smith and the Smiths' house. A year later, when Mrs. Smith's first baby was born, Biddy was the midwife—the person who helps the mother give birth. By this time, the Smiths could not manage without Biddy. They treated her well, for a slave, and did not whip her.

The Smiths had ten slaves, and one of their other slaves, Hannah, soon became Biddy's best friend. When their work was done for the day, Hannah and Biddy talked. Sometimes they ate their corn bread and catfish late at night, while the fire turned to gray ashes and the moon rolled across the sky.

Biddy had another friend, too; he was an Indian. Biddy often went to the marshy woods to gather plants and herbs for Mrs. Smith's medicine. It may be that she first met the Indian man in those woods, but nobody knows for sure. There were many Indians in Mississippi then—Choctaws, Cherokees, Chickasaws, and Creeks. Biddy's friend was the chief, or son of the chief, of one of these tribes, and family legend says they married. But Biddy was not free to choose a husband. She was Mr. Smith's slave. The Indian man soon disappeared from Biddy's life.

When Biddy was twenty, her first baby, Ellen, was born. By the time Biddy was thirty, she had three children: Ellen, age ten; Ann, age four, and Harriet, who was just a baby. (Family legend says the Indian man was Ellen's father. Mr. Smith may have been the father of Ann and Harriet.)

Biddy was strong, she was healthy, and she did every job she was told to do. She might have a better idea about how to do it, but she knew better than to say so. An "uppity" slave was whipped hard or maybe even sold and sent far away. Biddy wasn't uppity; she considered herself well treated, for a slave, and for a slave, she was.

Then, the year Biddy turned thirty, she left home again. But this time, everyone else left home too.

Leaving Mississippi

In the 1840s, Mormon missionaries came to Mississippi. Robert Smith liked what he heard of the new religion, and he and all his family became Mormons. Early in 1848, Smith, his wife's family, and four other white families in Mississippi decided to join other Mormons more than two thousand miles away in what would soon be the new Utah Territory. There they would be part of the Mormon "City of the Saints" by the Great Salt Lake.

Their guide, John Brown, wanted the Mississippi group to meet early in the spring at Fulton, Mississippi. From Fulton the six families would travel almost one thousand miles to the Mormon "Winter Quarters" on the west side of the Missouri River. At Winter Quarters, they would join a much larger wagon train to travel the remaining one thousand miles to Utah. Biddy heard that it might take more than half a year to get to Utah. She knew this wouldn't be easy.

Biddy was given a choice. She could stay in Mississippi as someone else's slave, or she could go with the Smiths. Biddy chose to stay with the owner she knew. Her friend Hannah chose the same. Mr. Smith could have taken their children, anyway, with or without Biddy and Hannah.

Biddy began getting the Smith family ready. She and the other slaves loaded three covered wagons with boxes of clothes and dishes; barrels of salt, sugar, cornmeal, rice, lard, beans, bacon, and raisins; iron cooking pots and tools. She hung the wooden butter churn on the end of a wagon. She found a place for Mrs. Smith's spinning wheel. Ten-year-old Ellen helped carry the Smiths' bedding and blankets to the wagons. Even little Ann ran back and forth, fetching boxes of matches and goose-feather pillows.

Mr. Smith's wagons headed north the first week of cool, rainy March. Biddy walked behind, keeping the cows and mules together. Morning and evening she milked the Smiths' seven cows. There would be plenty of milk and butter, she knew, as long as the cows had grass and water every night.

By March 9, all six families were in Fulton with their guide. Rainwater dripped from the rim of Mr. Brown's hat and off his bushy brown beard as he added Robert M. Smith's group to the list in his notebook: nine white people, ten black slaves, two yoke of oxen, one horse, eight mules, seven milk cows, three wagons.

It was still raining when they left Fulton, early in the morning on March 10. Biddy's hair and clothes were soaked, and her long skirt was covered with mud. Mud squished under her bare feet as she tried to keep Mr. Smith's cows and mules together behind the wagons. Ellen and Ann walked beside her. The three of them carried long sticks that they used to poke the cows that tried to stop to snatch mouthfuls of grass. Biddy carried baby Harriet, too, shifting her from arm to arm or tying the baby to her back.

Biddy and her girls weren't the only ones walking. Most of the white women and their children (but not the frail Mrs. Smith), and all the slaves, walked.

The white men sometimes rode horseback and sometimes walked, urging the oxen and mules on with their voices and their whips.

Mr. Brown called the wagons to a stop at noontime. "Nooning," he called it. It was a soggy nooning. Biddy didn't have to make a fire, though, since the noon meal was always breakfast leftovers. After she had helped the Smith family, Biddy sat with Hannah and their children on the wet grass. Biddy ate her corn bread, stretched her toes, and let her tired feet rest while the baby nursed.

They had gone twenty miles, Mr. Brown said, by the time the wagons camped that evening beside Bullmountain Stream. Ellen and Ann crawled under a wagon and lay side by side, as limp as rag dolls. Biddy was so tired she could scarcely lift her feet in the sticky mud, but there was more work to do.

She milked the cows, helped Mr. Smith get the animals tied up for the night, and helped Mrs. Smith feed her family. She got the Smiths' bedding ready. She put a pot of beans and bacon in the hot ashes to cook overnight. Then she fed Harriet and had another piece of corn bread and some milk from the pail. A handful of stars peeked around huge black clouds. More rain, Biddy thought, as she stretched out under the wagon with her girls.

A few stars still lingered when Mr. Brown hollered his wake-up holler. Biddy rolled out from under the wagon and carefully stood up. She was used to hard work and proud of how strong she was, but just then every muscle in her body hurt.

She ground the coffee beans and put the coffee on to boil. She milked the cows, poured the cream into the butter churn, and carried the milk pail to the Smiths' wagon. She and Hannah fried pork slices and cornmeal cakes. They dished up the beans and served the men first. By the time the men had the teams hitched up, Biddy had the iron skillet cleaned, breakfast put away, the fire out, and everybody ready to go.

Right away there was trouble. Bullmountain Stream was full of rushing water, and its bottom was pure, sticky mud. The heavy oak wheels of the first wagon got stuck in the boggy bottom of the stream. Water rushed under the wagon. It slapped against the bellies of the mules. But their feet might as well have been glued down.

Biddy helped lead four other mules into the stream and fastened them to the first team. She dragged the mules forward while the men pushed the wagon from behind. With a whooshing sound, the wheels pulled out of the mud and the wagon slowly rolled forward. By sundown all eleven wagons were on the other side.

It rained all night. Wind blew the rain under the canvas tops of the wagons and inside the slaves' tents. Biddy pushed her tent stakes into the mud and helped others whose tents were blowing away.

In the morning, the roads were as slippery as a greased possum. The oxen and mules pulling the wagons slipped; the cows and mules behind the wagons slipped; Biddy slipped. But they all got up again, coated with mud, and kept walking.

By the time they reached Lexington, Tennessee, twelve days later, Biddy had walked over one hundred miles. Her bare feet were tough, her legs were strong, and she was used to carrying Harriet while she drove the cows along. Biddy felt fine.

The oxen didn't feel fine, though. They often fell to their knees on the slippery roads. Stony roads cut their feet and muddy roads dragged on the wagon wheels. The oxen were exhausted. The mules didn't feel much better, and the journey had barely begun.

But every morning Mr. Brown gave his holler as soon as it was light enough to see his hand in front of his nose, and the wagons lurched forward. Day after day, Biddy sloshed through churned-up mud behind all the wagons and all the cows and mules she was driving. When they came to a river, she sent her animals in and plunged in after them.

Biddy couldn't remember when she had last worn dry clothes. It seemed as though she was either walking through pouring rain or swimming across a river. Either way she was as wet as a catfish.

On April 1, Biddy stood on the Kentucky side of the wide, ice-edged Ohio River—two miles wide and rising, Mr. Brown said. The rain poured down and the icy water rose higher and wider as Biddy tried to see the other side. She shivered and pulled her shawl tighter, her breath making little white clouds.

They had to cross the river, but the ferryboat wasn't working. Everyone and everything was wet and cold. Children whined and cried. Grown-ups shivered and worried. Finally Mr. Smith and others galloped off in the rain to find a boat.

Four miserable days later, Biddy heard shouting in the distance. Horses and mules whinnied as the men raced into camp, their wet saddles creaking. They had found a boat that would carry them from the Ohio River all the way up the Mississippi River to St. Louis.

Children stopped fussing and whooped with joy. Adults stopped worrying and gave thanks. Biddy sighed with relief. It was, she thought, more tiring to care for a sick woman and a wagonful of wet, whiny children than to walk twenty miles.

The next morning, Biddy helped load wagons, mules, oxen, and cows onto the boat. It was raining, as usual, and they were as wet as if they were *in* the river. Mr. Brown counted the people in his group, as usual, and wrote in his journal "30 whites [the Mormons] and 24 colored [the slaves]."

Biddy didn't have to work quite as hard once the boat pushed off. Mr. Smith's animals couldn't go anywhere and only needed to be fed and milked. She cooked, fetched, washed, and did everything the Smiths and their children needed or wanted. She cheerfully tended Hannah, who had just had a baby, and other slaves who were tired and sick.

And perhaps, for a few minutes each day, Biddy simply watched the muddy Mississippi River swirl by. Tree branches and even whole trees rose and fell in the water as the boat pushed its way north against the current. The river was so wide Biddy could barely see the far side. It was so quiet she could hear birds singing in the distant thick trees.

For a few days, Biddy could just stop and think. Perhaps she wondered if she and her daughters should have stayed in Mississippi. Probably she wondered how she would be asked to help the people she would meet in Utah Territory. Certainly she wondered what life would be like there.

They had almost reached St. Louis when the boat got stuck on a sandbar. There was only one thing to do—throw animals overboard until the boat floated higher. They threw twelve terrified mules into the river before the boat was free. But mules can swim, and they were happily eating grass by the time the boat's captain found a place to land (this time on purpose).

A few days later, the wagons rumbled west from St. Louis. Four hundred and fifty miles to Winter Quarters, and still they would not be even halfway to Utah.

The rain stopped as the wagon train plodded two hundred miles west toward the Missouri River. Wagon wheels and animal hooves turned the dry dirt into a cloud of dust which hung behind the wagons, right where Biddy was. She couldn't decide whether it was worse to be sloshing through the mud when it was raining, or to be in a dust cloud when it was dry. When they reached the Missouri River, the wagons turned north, to go two hundred and fifty miles beside the river to Kanesville (Council Bluffs), Iowa.

Finally, at the end of May, Biddy helped load wagons, animals, and people onto the ferryboats at Kanesville. They floated west across the Missouri River to the Mormon Winter Quarters in what would become Nebraska Territory, close by the Omaha Indian Reservation.

"My company has now gone 917 miles," Mr. Brown wrote in his journal. He wrote that they had had no deaths, one birth, and little sickness except a bit of chills and fever. He wrote that one ox had broken its neck. He didn't trouble to write how well Biddy had cared for the people in his company.

At Winter Quarters, Biddy's small group joined several hundred other people going to Utah. Biddy knew there was a long, hard walk ahead. There would be no stores where they could buy sugar or flour or salt or matches, if they ran out. She made sure the Smiths had everything they would need packed carefully into their wagons. She made sure the other slaves were as ready as they could be. She made sure her supply of plants and herbs was safely packed in her bag, probably including new plants she learned about from the Omaha Indians.

By the end of June, all the wagons were repaired, loaded, and ready to cross the prairie. On July 1, drivers shouted to their teams, children danced with excitement, and the whole company, Mr. Brown wrote, "moved on to the prairie."

3

Crossing the Prairie

The prairie was an ocean of grass. As the wind blew, the grass bowed down and rose up like waves at sea. The white canvas covers of the wagons bobbed back and forth like sailing ships. The grass was so tall in places that a person on horseback could get lost in it, but it became shorter and shorter the farther west the wagons moved.

Biddy tied a rag over her nose and mouth to keep the dust out and made Ellen and Ann do the same. She wore a sunbonnet to shade her face and neck from the blazing July sun. The stronger Mormon women, also wearing sunbonnets, walked beside their wagons to spare the oxen. Anyway, they said, it was more comfortable to walk than to ride inside the jolting, bake-oven wagons. The trail was right beside the Platte River, but the ground was as dry as a burr patch. Dust hung in the air where the wagons passed.

Day after day, the western prairie stretched before them like a vast tabletop, and heat waves rose up as if from a sizzling skillet. Day after day, the oxen plodded on, and the wagons rumbled forward on squeaking wheels.

Biddy and her daughters were soaked with sweat, covered with mosquito bites, and caked with dust. They ran back and forth to keep the cows and mules together and going in the right direction.

Sometimes Biddy asked Ellen and Ann to watch their little sister. Harriet could toddle along the trail now, slowly, and Ellen and Ann had to be sure she didn't fall under a heavy wooden wagon wheel or put her small hand into a rattlesnake's hole. Biddy had already seen graves by the trail. She promised herself and her girls that they would get to Utah safely.

Every night when her work was done, and she had checked that all was well with the wagons and the people in them, Biddy lay on her blanket and looked at the stars flung out over the great black sky. Far away, wolves howled. Close by, coyotes barked. Biddy's eyes closed. And then, it seemed, no sooner had she fallen asleep than the morning bugle sounded for prayers, and the day began all over again.

Biddy's job herding the animals became harder the farther west they traveled. Each day the sun blazed hotter, the grass was sparser, and the animals were more thirsty and hungry. The only rest came when they nooned in the shade of the cottonwoods along the murmuring Platte River.

After more days of walking, the prairie grass came to an end, and the dry ground was dotted with sage-brush and cactus. The cows began dying, and Biddy could not help them. The wagons pushed on through the sand hills, leaving behind dead cows for the wolves and vultures.

Then one August morning, Biddy saw mountains far off in the distance, and the rising sun glowed pink on the first snowy peaks Biddy had ever seen. Days later the wagons rolled into Fort Laramie, in Wyoming Territory.

From Fort Laramie, the wagon train began the last part of the journey. Biddy drove the animals over high deserts and mountains, through meadows of flowers, and past rock-filled streams that ran along the bottom of narrow canyons.

The wagon train climbed the rocky Wasatch moun-tains. The rain on Biddy's face felt colder and colder the higher they climbed. Before long the rain turned to a storm of icy sleet and snow. The oxen slipped and crashed to their knees as they leaned forward, try-ing to pull the wagons up the muddy, freezing trail.

Ellen and Ann were so tired that Biddy held their hands and pulled them along with her behind the staggering animals, while Harriet clung to her back. She heard sobs from the weary women plodding along beside the wagons ahead.

In the first week of October, Biddy and her girls stood with the other exhausted pioneers on the last mountaintop and looked down into a wide valley with a vivid blue lake. Songs, prayers, and shouts of joy filled the clear air. Biddy hugged her girls tight. They were almost there!

Now the wagons bounced down the steep mountain. They skidded between boulders and rocks, oak trees and pine trees. The drivers clung desperately to ropes and chains, trying to keep their wagons from hurtling away from them. Smoke curled up from the wooden brakes pressing on the wheels. Grasshoppers and crickets whirred up in Biddy's face as she slid down the mountain behind the wagons, clinging to bushes and branches. Her girls slipped and tumbled behind her.

At the foot of the mountain, they struggled through one last canyon, and then the wide valley was in front of them. The Great Salt Lake lay like a blue-silver band in the distance. Ribbons of steam rose from hot springs far to the north.

Biddy heard shouts from the front of the wagon train. Mormon pioneers who had made the very first journey the year before were coming to meet them. The shouts passed down the whole train, and suddenly men, women, and children were screaming, crying, dancing, even fainting from excitement. They had done it!

Biddy didn't scream or cry or faint, but she surely felt like dancing. She had brought her daughters, and every other person she was responsible for, safely all the way.

Biddy, her girls, and the whole wagon train camped in Emigration Canyon, outside Great Salt Lake City. The next morning, the Smiths and their slaves and most of those in John Brown's group moved to a huge empty space between two tall cottonwood trees on Cottonwood Creek. There—two thousand miles and seven months from Mississippi—they stopped. The journey was over.

⟫◆⟪

Now the pioneers had to get ready for winter in their new settlement by the cottonwoods. Slave and Mormon men chopped down trees, sawed up logs, and built log cabins in the cold November sunshine and even colder rain.

Biddy unpacked the barrels and boxes; she washed the prairie mud and sand out of the Smiths' clothes; she heated the flatiron and ironed the clothes; she carried pots and pans, bedding, and Mrs. Smith's spinning wheel into the Smiths' new log cabin. (Biddy and her daughters probably had a little log cabin of their own behind the Smiths' cabin, as a few other slaves did.)

At Cottonwood Creek, there were several Mississippi families with slaves. The Mormon Church in Utah had no law about slavery, and church leaders weren't sure what to do about the slaves. Finally they decided that if a slave wished to leave his or her master, the master must let the slave go in peace. But, the Mormon leaders added, "all the slaves that are there appear to be perfectly contented and satisfied."

It's not known if Mr. Smith told his slaves they could choose to leave. Probably he didn't. None of them left, and Biddy and her friend Hannah both remained slaves to the Smith family. Biddy had many responsibilities to manage for the Smiths, and she was happiest when she could do things for them and for others. Biddy's daughters were growing up healthy and strong, just like their mother. Biddy still thought she and her girls were all well treated, for slaves.

Hannah thought the same. It's also likely that Mr. Smith was the father of Hannah's children, too.

Life was hard at Cottonwood Creek. Grasshoppers ate every single thing they could, from vegetable gardens to plow handles. The summers were fearfully hot and dry. Salt and scratchy dust hurt Biddy's throat and made her girls cough. In winter the icy winds were so fierce that salt spray from the lake blew all the way into Great Salt Lake City, twelve miles away, and snow stayed for months.

But when spring came, Biddy went out looking for new plants and herbs for her medicine bag and her garden. The mountain streams were so clear she could see the pebbles on the bottom. Quaking aspen trees stood in groups, with silvery green leaves and bark as white as paper. The riverbanks were covered with willows, birch trees, tall pines, and brilliant red maples. Biddy thought her new home was beautiful.

She was surprised, three years later, when Mr. Smith said they were moving on again.

4

To California and Freedom

They were going to move almost eight hundred miles to California. Four hundred Mormons, including Robert M. Smith, were to start a new Mormon settlement close to the little village of Los Angeles. There they would plant crops and "moral values."

The Smith family, their slaves, and all their animals left Salt Lake City in March 1851. They joined a long train of one hundred and fifty wagons headed south, toward Los Angeles. Biddy walked behind the Smiths' wagons, as before, herding the animals. But this time she didn't have to carry Harriet. Harriet was three years old, Ann was seven, and Ellen was a teenager of thirteen.

At first the trip was easy. So many men had rushed to the California goldfields in 1849 that the trail was well marked, with good places to camp.

All went well for almost two hundred miles. Then Biddy saw the wagons in front heading straight into the mountains. They climbed up, down, and up again. Days later the wagons bounced down the mountains and creaked into a river valley.

The wagons crawled up more mountains and across a desert. They crossed into California and another desert. They kept moving all night, trying to reach water. Some of the oxen couldn't pull any longer. Some were too weak to stand. Biddy tried not to watch as the men shot animals that had walked obediently all the way from Utah.

The wagon train left the Mojave Desert behind at last and trudged up into the San Gabriel Mountains. Finally, on an evening in early June, the wagons rumbled down out of the mountains and into a wide valley. Biddy caught her breath at its gentle beauty. The valley stretched out far in the distance, with vineyards and fruit trees. Great herds of cattle and horses grazed on the soft green hills. The wagon train stopped. This would be Biddy's new home.

Biddy, age thirty-three, and her daughters settled into life in the new log cabin town of San Bernardino.

Here the Mormons and their slaves raised corn, wheat, vegetables, and chickens. Rebecca Smith was still sickly, and now she had six children. Biddy helped run the Smith household, care for the Smith children, and fetch and carry for Mrs. Smith. It was much more pleasant to be a "pampered house slave," as Biddy said she was, than a mule driver. It was much easier than walking miles every day in a dust cloud or a rainstorm. It was much better than climbing mountains or slipping and crashing down stony trails.

Most of Biddy's days were filled by other people's needs. But on Sundays, when she had some time for herself, Biddy probably took her daughters with her to explore the hills around San Bernardino. She found new plants and herbs to use in making medicines. She showed her daughters how to choose just the right plants, as her slave teachers back in Mississippi had shown her.

It might be, on those walks, that Biddy thought about freedom. During the journey from Utah, she had met two black people in the wagon train who were not slaves. Elizabeth and Charles Rowan were free blacks, going to California because they wanted to. Elizabeth had been freed by her Mormon master, and she had met and married Charles in Utah. It was possible, Biddy realized, to be black and not a slave.

By 1855 Biddy was beginning to think more about being free. She talked about freedom with her daughters, Ellen, age seventeen, Ann, age eleven, and Harriet, age seven. She talked with Hannah, with other slaves, and with people who were already free. What would it mean? Biddy wondered. Where would they go? But she waited and thought some more.

Biddy had met several black people in San Bernardino and Los Angeles who were not slaves. She met Robert Owens, a wealthy black businessman and property owner, and his wife, Winnie. She learned that California was not a slave state—it had been admitted to the Union as a free state in 1850. Two years before that California had been part of Mexico, so people were confused about the rules. Sometimes it seemed that Mexican law, military law, and California law were all in force at the same time. But there was no doubt about one thing—California was not a slave state.

Robert Smith was worried. He had assumed things would stay as they always had. But he knew that Biddy knew she was in a free state and that she was talking about it with the other slaves. At the end of 1855, he made plans to take his family and slaves to Texas, a slave state. In Texas there wouldn't be any foolish talk of slaves leaving their master.

Meanwhile, Biddy's daughter Ellen and Robert Owens's son Charles had fallen in love. When Charles heard that Mr. Smith was planning to leave California, taking Ellen away, he told his father.

At the same time, Biddy herself told Robert Owens and Elizabeth Rowan about Smith's plan. She feared the trip to Texas, she said, even though Mr. Smith promised she'd always be well treated.

For nineteen years, Biddy had obeyed her master. She had walked behind his wagons for thousands of miles, from Mississippi to Salt Lake City to San Bernardino. But now Biddy knew she and her daughters could be free, and she made up her mind. She would *not* leave California.

Mr. Owens and Mrs. Rowan went straight to the Los Angeles County sheriff. They told him that Smith was planning to take slaves out of California. In fact, Smith was already camped in the Santa Monica Mountains with his family and his fourteen slaves, on their way to Texas.

The sheriff rode to Smith's camp. He accused Smith of trying to persuade "persons of color to go out of the State of California." He took Biddy, Hannah, and their children to the county jail "for their protection." Biddy feared what Mr. Smith might do next. He would have to go to court to get his slaves back.

In January Judge Benjamin Hayes heard the case in the Los Angeles County Courthouse. In court Mr. Smith told Judge Hayes that Biddy and Hannah had agreed to leave Mississippi with him, that they were not slaves, but members of his family, and that he kept them in "no greater control than his own children." Some of this was true, since the slave children probably *were* his children. Smith said that Hannah was "well disposed" to stay with him and that this was all Biddy's idea.

Judge Hayes considered Biddy the leader of the group, but under California law she was not permitted to speak in court because she was black. In the judge's office, where Biddy was allowed to speak, she said, "I have always done what I have been told to do." She said she feared the trip to Texas even though Mr. Smith had told her she "would be just as free in Texas as here."

Then Hannah's daughter Ann asked Judge Hayes, "Will I be as free in Texas as here?"

Judge Hayes knew they would not be free at all. He thought the only reason Smith wanted to take fourteen slaves (Biddy and her three girls, Hannah and her nine children and grandchildren) to Texas was to sell them. He thought that Biddy feared the trip because she knew "she would again be a slave."

Now Mr. Smith was even more worried. He bribed the court lawyer who spoke for the slaves, giving him $100 to quit the case. Judge Hayes found out about the bribe. At the same time, he decided that Biddy and the other slaves wanted to stay in California, but they were afraid to stand up to Mr. Smith.

On January 21, 1856, Judge Hayes ruled that "all the said persons of color . . . are entitled to their freedom and are free forever." The former slaves, he said, should "go to work for themselves—in peace and without fear." Then he ordered Mr. Smith to pay all the court costs. This was too much for Mr. Smith. He fled California, without his slaves, and without paying the costs.

Hannah took the last name Smith and returned to San Bernardino. Biddy did exactly what Judge Hayes said to do—she went to work for herself, in peace and without fear. But first, she needed a last name of her own and a place to stay. She took the name Mason, perhaps from one of the Mormon trailblazers, and for the rest of her life was Biddy Mason. Then she accepted Robert Owens's offer to stay with his family in Los Angeles.

She had three daughters to care for. She did not have one penny. But she had a plan.

On Her Own

Except for her friends, Biddy Mason was on her own. She wasn't worried. Her former master had left California, she had the paper from Judge Hayes that said she was free, and she knew how to care for sick people. She quickly found a job as a nurse and midwife for Dr. John S. Griffin of Los Angeles. Dr. Griffin knew both Robert Owens and Judge Hayes, so he had heard about Biddy's nursing skills. He paid her $2.50 a day (a good salary, when a boardinghouse meal cost about 50¢). Biddy saved every penny she could, to someday buy a home of her own.

She walked everywhere she could, too. Ordinary folks rode in *carretas*—heavy, squealing, two-wheeled wooden carts pulled by oxen or horses. Rich folks rode in fancy carriages. Most men rode horseback. But Biddy had walked thousands of miles already, from Mississippi to Utah to California. Walking around the dusty streets of small-town Los Angeles was nothing to her.

The wide dirt streets had no sidewalks when Biddy first arrived. She, and everyone else on foot, walked in the street. This wasn't too bad except in the rainy season. Then the streets turned to mud, two feet deep. And when it was dry, which was most of the time, Biddy often found herself in a dust cloud.

Dust swirled up from the galloping hooves of the spirited horses ridden by Californios, rich Mexicans who owned the huge cattle ranches of Southern California. The Californios dashed through the wide, empty streets as if they owned them—until 1859, when a new law was passed against riding in the city "at a furious rate."

Spanish was the language of Los Angeles in the 1850s, and Biddy must have learned it. She helped Mexicans and Indians, black people and white people. She nursed people in the county jail and in the new county hospital. She went wherever she was needed.

She had herbs and medicines in her big black bag, and gentleness in her touch. Biddy's patients did well, and sick people and mothers having babies wanted her with them. They said she had the gift of healing in her hands.

Biddy walked from the large old adobes of wealthy Mexican ranchers, to the small wooden houses of new Anglos from the United States, to the smaller shacks of Indians working in the vineyards and orange groves. While she was at a sick person's house, she also helped by cooking and cleaning. She also might look after the older children of a mother who had just had another baby.

Often the poorest people (people who were not Dr. Griffin's patients) could only pay Biddy with some bread or vegetables or a chicken. Some could pay nothing. Biddy helped anyway. She told her daughters that a person must give with open hands and an open heart, and she showed them how to do it.

Biddy's daughter Ellen married Charles Owens soon after she got her freedom. Ellen and Charles moved to a small house close to Robert Owens's family, and Biddy rented a small white house with a picket fence, close to them all.

Biddy and her daughters were just getting used to their new life when the worst thing that could happen, happened. Thirteen-year-old Ann died in 1857 from an infection. By mistake, she had jumped into a dirty watering trough for horses. Ann had crossed rivers, prairies, mountains, and deserts beside her mother, and now she was dead. Biddy had a great sadness in her heart for the rest of her life, but she knew she had to keep going.

Biddy's first grandson, Robert, was born in 1858. Two years later Biddy had another grandson, Henry. Her family was growing, and so was Los Angeles.

Los Angeles now had some office buildings, one brick sidewalk, and a few more rules to control the people, but no one could control the weather. In 1861 there was a whole month of rain. There were mud holes in the streets deep enough to drown a man. Dead dogs, dead cats, and dead chickens floated in the ditches. Wherever Biddy walked, the smell of death was in her nose.

Shocking news came in 1861 from President Abraham Lincoln in Washington. His message was sent by Pony Express to San Francisco and then by telegraph to Los Angeles. President Lincoln said the Southern states wanted to leave the United States and be a separate, slaveholding country—but he told the South that the Union must stay together. So the Southern and Northern states were at war.

People in Los Angeles lived far from the war, but everyone, except the Mexicans and the Indians, had come from either the North or the South. Many people, including Dr. Griffin, supported the South. Biddy did not say out loud what she thought but went about her business. And her business was to help people who were sick.

The very next year, smallpox, a horrible and deadly disease, appeared in Los Angeles. Not many people were willing to help those who were sick and dying from smallpox. The Catholic Sisters of Charity, who had opened the first hospital in Los Angeles in 1857, helped. And Biddy Mason helped. She took her black bag, risked her life, and walked right past the yellow warning flags on sick people's houses. She didn't catch smallpox, and she saved the lives of many who had it.

While Biddy worked to save lives, thousands were dying in the Civil War between North and South. The South, Biddy's old home, was a battlefield. In 1863 President Lincoln's Emancipation Proclamation freed the slaves in the rebelling states. In 1865 the North finally won the war. The United States stayed united, but President Lincoln was dead. He was killed one week after war ended, by a man who thought the South should have won.

When the news of President Lincoln's death reached Los Angeles in April 1865, Biddy and her family probably had a private memorial at home. Biddy probably talked about her life as a slave in the South and gave thanks that there were no more slaves there, only free people. By the end of 1865, *every* American slave was free.

Biddy had used her own freedom to save her money, penny by penny, until she had $250. This wasn't enough money to buy land in downtown Los Angeles, by the Plaza, but Biddy could buy property farther away. In 1866 she bought land one mile south of town, on Third and Spring Streets, where there were lots of vineyards, orange trees, and gardens. Her land had "a ditch of water" and a "willow fence," and Biddy loved it. She told her daughters it was always to remain as their homestead, no matter whether they were rich or poor. All her life she called it "the Homestead."

Biddy had two houses built on her new land, but she didn't move in, yet. She liked the house she was renting close to the two Owens families and her grandsons, so she stayed there and rented her houses to other people. She kept saving her money. Before long, she had enough to buy more land around Sixth and Olive Streets for $375.

Los Angeles was growing like a patch of summer weeds. Now, if Biddy walked home after sunset, she saw the lamplighter on his horse, lighting the new gas lamps on street corners. For 10¢, Biddy could ride in a horsecar all the way from Sixth and Spring to the new three-story hotels on the Plaza. She probably saved her money, though, and walked.

She was glad that the long mule trains clattered up Main Street, a block away, instead of Spring Street. The stagecoach dashed up Main Street, too, with its sweating horses puffing and snorting. The driver blew a small trumpet to warn grown-ups, little children, chickens, and dogs to jump out of the way. Even more exciting, sometimes two coaches raced each other to see who could get to the hotels first.

Long lines of covered wagons parked on Main Street, while newcomers tried to figure out where to go first. Flocks of sheep, lumbering oxen, barking dogs, saddle horses, farm wagons, and Chinese men carrying boxes hung from bamboo poles appeared and disappeared through clouds of dust. If she wanted to, Biddy could buy fruit, peanuts, tortillas, iced lemonade, or beef cooked over charcoal from peddlers pushing carts. By the end of the day, Biddy's ears hurt from the shouting and banging and clattering, and her lungs hurt from the dust and smoke.

In 1870 there were fewer than one hundred black people in Los Angeles. Most of the men worked as blacksmiths, farmers, or wagon drivers. Most of the women worked as maids for white families. Biddy probably knew them all. She talked with her old friend Winnie Owens (Robert Owens had died in 1865), and others, about starting a new black church. In 1872 twelve people, including Winnie Owens and Ellen and Charles, met in Biddy's home to make plans. When the meeting was over, they had formed the Los Angeles branch of the First African Methodist Episcopal Church, or FAME. The new church would meet in Biddy's home until the members could afford their own building.

As Biddy walked through Los Angeles carrying her nursing bag, it seemed as though the city grew in front of her eyes. She saw more hotels, an elementary school, a high school, a university, a public library, a cathedral, a teachers' college, and a park at Pershing Square. A city hall was built on Spring and Jail Streets (the city jail was right behind). And if there was a fire in one of the many wooden buildings in Los Angeles, galloping horses (or sometimes the firefighters themselves) pulled two shiny red fire engines with polished brass trim from Engine Company #1 and Engine Company #2.

By the 1880s, Biddy's block on Spring Street was filled with businesses—furniture and grocery stores, bakeries and offices. Biddy's grandsons, Robert and Henry, wanted to start a business, too. So Biddy loaned them part of her property for a livery stable. Soon many of the horses trotting up and down the streets of Los Angeles stayed at Owens' Bros. Livery & Feed. Biddy was proud to see their stable doing so well, and a few years later she sold the property to them for "the sum of love and affection and ten dollars."

Spring Street wasn't a street for little houses anymore. By 1884 Biddy had sold part of her land for $2,800 and had a two-story building of her own put up on another part. The first floor was rented out for storage, and the second floor was her home.

Then she sold a bit more land for even more money. And then a bit more for still more money. People were pouring into Los Angeles like a flood. Los Angeles was spreading south, and Biddy's land on Spring Street was in the middle of it. Her land was worth a fortune.

Biddy Mason was a rich woman. In fact, she was one of the richest women in Los Angeles. She could stop working, if she wanted. She could buy clothes and jewels, if she wanted. But that wasn't Biddy's way.

With Open Hands

Biddy Mason did not want to sit at home. She did not want to buy things for herself. She wanted to help others. She didn't stop taking care of other people; she did more of it, and she became the center of the black community in Los Angeles.

In 1884 there was another long rainstorm, and the Los Angeles River turned into a raging torrent. People who lived beside the river saw their houses and everything they owned disappear.

Biddy didn't wait for someone else to help. She went straight to her neighborhood grocery store on Fourth and Spring Streets and opened an account.

When someone comes in who needs food and can't pay, she said, put it on this account. *I* will pay, she said. It didn't matter to Biddy whether the person was black or white. What mattered was that the person needed help.

Ten years before, Biddy had helped to start the FAME church. All these years, Biddy had made sure the taxes and the minister were paid; she paid them herself if the church couldn't. Now she also paid the taxes for other churches in need, but she didn't keep a record of how much money she spent, or for which church. She just quietly paid the amount needed. And it didn't matter who went to the church; what mattered was that the church needed help. Word spread that Biddy Mason was a person of open hands and a generous spirit.

Some of the new white people coming to Los Angeles thought they were better than the black people who lived there. They said black people were not welcome in their churches and clubs and hotels. Biddy Mason, who was one of the "best" people in Los Angeles, wanted to be sure this idea didn't catch on. Perhaps because of this, she often went to Sunday service at the mostly white Fort Street Methodist Episcopal Church, which was right across the street from her homestead.

Unfortunately, this idea *did* catch on. The FAME church had bought property on Fourth and Charity Streets for $700 and put up a small building. FAME rented this building to the Board of Education from Monday through Friday as an elementary school for black children. But they were forced to leave because of angry white people who lived nearby.

Biddy kept nursing and caring for people who needed her, and now she could do it for free. She taught other women how to use a gentle touch and calming voice as part of their nursing tools. Long before the first black student was allowed into the nursing school at the Los Angeles County Hospital, Biddy Mason taught nursing and midwifery in Los Angeles.

Almost every day, Biddy packed little gifts of food in her basket and walked to the jail behind the courthouse. Biddy remembered how she had felt when the sheriff put her in jail to protect her from Mr. Smith, and her heart hurt for the men there. She prayed with them and talked with them about why they were in jail, so it wouldn't happen again. She was known as "a frequent visitor to the jail," and the men welcomed her cheerful spirit. They called her "Grandma Mason." In fact, she was so well known in Los Angeles, especially in the poorer parts of town, that *most* folks called her Grandma Mason.

No one had noticed that black children needed nursery schools and day care centers—until Biddy Mason did. Right in her own neighborhood she started a school and a day care center for black children and for any child who had nowhere else to go.

Some grown-ups had nowhere to go, too. Biddy, who still greeted the world with open hands, took people in need into her home. She gave them food and let them rest. It didn't matter who the person was; what mattered was that the person needed help.

Every morning a line of people seeking help waited outside Biddy's door. As she grew older, her grandsons tried to spare her by turning people away. But until the day she couldn't get out of bed, Biddy welcomed people into her home.

⬥

Biddy Mason died on January 15, 1891. Her funeral service was held at the Fort Street Church, and she was buried without fuss. She was laid to rest in Evergreen Cemetery in an unmarked grave.

Biddy's family remembers a saying she passed down to them. "If you hold your hand closed," Biddy said, "nothing good can come in. The open hand is blessed, for it gives in abundance, even as it receives." All her life, Biddy Mason believed this. All her life, Biddy Mason gave in abundance.

Afterword

Because Biddy Mason did her work and gave her gifts quietly, many people did not know of her goodness and of the wonderful gifts that flowed from her hands. But that is changing.

On March 27, 1988, Los Angeles Mayor Tom Bradley, three thousand members of the FAME church, and members of Biddy Mason's family placed an impressive tombstone over her grave. And on November 16, 1989, a Biddy Mason memorial wall was unveiled on the site of her former homestead on Third and Spring Streets in downtown Los Angeles. The city declared this day to be Biddy Mason Day in Los Angeles.

Biddy Mason gave with open hands and an open heart to any person in need. Her life is a gift to us all.

Bibliography

Beasley, Delilah L. *The Negro Trail Blazers of California.* 1919. Reprint, New York: Negro Universities Press, 1969.

Biddy Mason Papers. University of California Los Angeles, Research Library, Special Collections.

Brown, John. *Autobiography of Pioneer John Brown, 1820–1896.* Salt Lake City, Utah: 1941.

Bunch, Lonnie G., III. *Black Angelenos: The Afro-American in Los Angeles, 1850–1950.* Exhibition catalog. Los Angeles: California Afro-American Museum, 1989.

"California Freedom Papers." *Journal of Negro History* (January 1918).

Hayden, Dolores. "Biddy Mason's Los Angeles 1856-1891." *California History* (Fall 1989).

Hayes, Judge Benjamin I. "Suit for Freedom." *Los Angeles Star* (February 2, 1856).

Hine, Darlene Clark, editor. *Black Women in America.* Volume II. Brooklyn, N.Y.: Carlson Publishing Inc., 1993.

Latter-Day Saints in El Dorado: The Mormon Presence in California, 1846–1856. Exhibition. Huntington Library, San Marino, California. August 1997.

"Mississippi Company, 1848." *Our Pioneer Heritage.* Volume 8. Salt Lake City, Utah: Daughters of the Utah Pioneers, 1965.

Mungen, Donna. *Life and Times of Biddy Mason.* MC Printing Company, funded by The California Arts Council, 1976.

Smith, Jessie Carney, editor. *Epic Lives: One Hundred Black Women Who Made a Difference.* Detroit, Mich.: Visible Ink Press, 1993.

Smith, Jessie Carney, editor. *Notable Black American Women.* Detroit, Mich.: Gale Research Inc., 1992.

Spalding, William A. *History and Reminiscences Los Angeles City and County California.* Volume I. Los Angeles: J.R. Finnell & Sons, undated.

"The Negro Woman in LA and Vicinity: Some Notable Characters." *LA Daily Times* (February 12, 1909).

Thurman, Sue. *Pioneers of Negro Origin in California.* San Francisco: Acme Publishing Co., 1952.

Wood, Brent A. "First African Methodist Episcopal Church and Its Social Intervention in South Central Los Angeles." Doctoral dissertation, University of Southern California, 1997. Used by permission.

Websites

http://members.tripod.com/~bobij   Learn about Biddy Mason's contributions to Los Angeles history at this Website created by historian Bobi Jackson.

http://206.83.187.33/pioneer/biddy.htm   Journalist LeAnne von Neumeyer writes about Biddy Mason's Mormon past.

Index

Bradley, Los Angeles Mayor Tom, 59
Brown, John, 15, 16, 17, 18, 20, 21, 23, 25, 31
Brown, Linda Spikes Cox (great-great-great-granddaughter), 6
Bullmountain Stream, 17, 18

California, 35, 36, 37, 38, 39, 40, 42, 43, 44
Californios, 44
Civil War, 47, 48
Cottonwood Creek, Utah, 31, 33, 34

Emancipation Proclamation, 48
Emigration Canyon, Utah, 31

First African Methodist Episcopal Church (FAME), 51, 55, 56, 59
Fort Laramie, Wyo., 29
Fort Street Methodist Episcopal Church, 55, 58
Fulton, Miss., 15, 16

Georgia, 7, 9
Great Salt Lake, Utah, 14, 30
Great Salt Lake City, Utah. See Salt Lake City, Utah
Griffin, Dr. John S., 43, 46, 48

Hannah. See Smith, Hannah

Hayes, Judge Benjamin, 40, 42, 43

Indians, 13, 24, 25, 44, 46, 48

Kanesville (Council Bluffs), Iowa, 24

Latter-day Saints, Church of. See Mormons
Lexington, Tenn., 20
Lincoln, President Abraham, 47, 48–49
Los Angeles, Calif., 35, 38, 42, 43, 44, 48, 49, 53, 56, 59: and African Americans, 51, 54, 55, 58; growth of, 47, 50, 51
Los Angeles County sheriff, 39
Los Angeles River, 54

Mason, Ann (daughter), 13, 15, 16, 17, 27, 28, 30, 35, 38, 40, 47
Mason, Bridget "Biddy:" birth, 7, 9; charity, 7, 54–55, 56, 58, 59; death, 58; and freedom, 37, 38, 39, 40, 42; and money, 7, 42, 43, 46, 49, 50, 53, 55, 56; nursing skills, 10, 11, 23, 43, 44–46, 48, 56; "open hand" philosophy, 7, 46, 58; and slavery, 10, 13, 15, 33, 37, 38, 40, 49

62

Mason, Ellen (daughter), 13,
15, 16, 17, 27, 28, 30, 35,
38, 39, 46, 51
Mason, Harriet (daughter), 13,
16, 17, 20, 28, 30, 35, 38
Mexicans, 44, 46, 48. *See
also* Californios
Mexico, 38
Mississippi, 9, 14, 15, 23, 31,
33, 37, 39, 40, 44
Mississippi River, 21, 23
Missouri River, 15, 24
Mojave Desert, 36
Mormons, 14, 15, 23, 24, 27,
31, 33, 35, 37, 42

Native Americans. *See* Indians
Nebraska Territory, 24

Ohio River, 21
Owens' Bros. Livery & Feed,
53
Owens, Charles (son-in-law),
39, 46, 51
Owens, Ellen Mason. *See*
Mason, Ellen
Owens, Henry (grandson), 47,
53
Owens, Robert, 38, 39, 42, 43,
46, 51
Owens, Robert (grandson), 47,
53
Owens, Winnie, 38, 51

Platte River, 27, 29

Rowan, Charles, 37
Rowan, Elizabeth, 37, 39

Salt Lake City, Utah, 31, 34,
35, 39
San Bernadino, Calif., 36, 37,
38, 39, 42
San Francisco, Calif., 47
San Gabriel Mountains, 36
Santa Monica Mountains, 39
Sisters of Charity, 48
Smith, Hannah, 11, 15, 17, 18,
23, 33, 34, 38, 39, 40, 42
Smith, Rebecca, 11, 13, 15,
16, 33, 37
Smith, Robert M., 11, 13, 16,
17, 21, 23, 33, 34, 35, 38,
39, 40, 42, 56: conversion to
Mormonism, 14; marriage,
11; slave children, 13, 15,
34, 40
Smithson, John, 9, 11
St. Louis, Mo., 21, 24

Texas, 38, 39, 40

Union, the, 38, 47
United States. *See* Union, the
Utah Territory, 14, 15, 23, 24,
25, 28, 33, 36, 37, 44

Wasatch mountains, 29
Washington, D.C., 47
Winter Quarters, 15, 24, 25
Wyoming Territory, 29

About the Author

Jeri Chase Ferris is a native Nebraskan whose love of history comes from her prairie roots. For many years, however, she has lived in Los Angeles, where she was an elementary school teacher for almost thirty years.

As a teacher, she regretted the absence of information for children and adults about Biddy Mason's role in early Los Angeles. As an author, she has begun to fill the gap.

Ms. Ferris and her husband, Tom, a teacher and historian, have two grown sons and four perfect grandchildren. They enjoy traveling worldwide and they collaborate on Russian-American writing projects.

About the Illustrator

Ralph L. Ramstad feels lucky to have had the opportunity to illustrate the life of Biddy Mason. "This is a person who gives meaning to the words *strong* and *character!*" Mr. Ramstad says. "I hope my drawings help to make this remarkable woman alive and real to young people of today."

Mr. Ramstad studied at the Pratt Institute in Brooklyn, New York. For 42 years, he created art for product packaging, print advertisements, and billboards. Mr. Ramstad has also illustrated *The Flight of the Union, Birds in the Bushes: A Story about Margaret Morse Nice,* and *The Back of Beyond: A Story about Lewis and Clark,* all published by Carolrhoda Books. He lives in Minneapolis, Minnesota, with his wife.